Girls, Girls, Girls

A reconstructive surgery for misogyny in 8 songs

Anna McKerrow

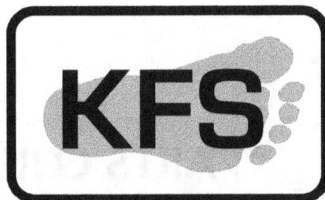

KFS

Newton-le-Willows

Published in the United Kingdom in 2019
by The Knives Forks And Spoons Press,
51 Pipit Avenue,
Newton-le-Willows,
Merseyside,
WA12 9RG.

ISBN 978-1-912211-48-7

Supported using public funding by

ARTS COUNCIL ENGLAND

LOTTERY FUNDED

CÖNTËNTS

Foreword   5

Notes on the Poems   7

Bones   13

Apple Pie Tattoo   15

Five Years Uptown   17

Girls, Girls, Girls   27

Forward my Mail to Me in Hell   37

(All in) the Name of the Father   43

She Plays the Role of a Roving Matriarch   45

You're All I(ncel) Need   55

FÖREWÖRD

Mötley Crüe's fourth studio album, *Girls, Girls, Girls*, was released on my tenth birthday in 1987. It reached number 2 in the US Billboard 200 Chart that year and sold over 4 million copies in the US, and 60,000 in the UK. In it, the band, notorious by that time for their drink-and-drug-fuelled rock n'roll lifestyle, included songs about their drug and stripper-loving lifestyle.

This work seeks to restructure the *Girls, Girls, Girls* album, not to *reveal* its inherent misogyny – that should be apparent by listening to the lyrics – but to make something of them.

As a *girl* child who would grow up to be a *Girl* in the Mötley Crüe sense of the word, I received their messaging about what a girl was – a passive sexual object to be desired and abused – along with a raft of variously textured misogyny in TV advertising, film, other music, magazines, print media and the attitudes and assumptions of the adults around me. I took in the *Girls, Girls, Girls* album as a model of what being a Girl was, in my little town in the west country, far away from the Sunset Strip.

I was wrong to do so, of course, but what did I know? I loved metal bands, and thought they were lewd and wild and marvellous. But despite its title, *Girls, Girls, Girls* was never meant for me: the songs on it, and on most albums in the genre produced and made by men, were made for a male, heterosexual audience. Perhaps no-one – the producers, the marketers, the band themselves – ever thought about their teenage girl fans, unless it was to decide which ones in the crowd they wanted to sleep with at a concert. It was, therefore, a very good thing that the Riot Grrrl movement came along in the 90s, to *liberate us girls from male, white, corporate oppression* (Sonic Youth, *Kool Thing*, 1990).

Mötley Crüe were by no means alone in perpetuating misogynist attitudes towards women in the 80s and 90s, and on an individual level, it could be said that they were mostly concerned with getting high and having as much sex as humanly possible – and were not actively pursuing personal misogynist agendas (though, some responsibility does of course have to rest on their shoulders).

More, they were a hugely successful band making ideological content encouraged by the patriarchal structures that contracted them to do so – the commercial music industry, which, like all capitalist, commercial cultural production industries, aims to uphold and regulate the social norms in which it operates, thereby ensuring continued investment in its business.

Girls, Girls, Girls absolutely typifies the apotheosis of misogyny in a variety of ways. First, it *looks at* women as objects rather than converses with them in a meaningful way. Second, it considers women only as lovers for heterosexual men. Third, it depicts unrealistic, patriarchally-approved female bodies. Fourth, it alludes to sex with underage girls, which is rape. Fifth, in songs like *You're All I Need*, desire for women is tied up closely with violence towards them, something I explore against the current narrative of the 'incel' movement.

The only song on the album that I haven't included is *Nona*, which is a short, one-line song, but which deserves mention as the one tiny song-ette that actually addresses a real woman, mourning the sudden death of one of the band members' grandmothers. Ironically, of course, the only time that a real woman is referred to she is dead.

To make the poems in this collection I have used a few different approaches, namely cutup with other sources to provide commentary and comment on the original song lyrics, breaking down the songs to component words and rewriting them, and finding recurrent themes, such as that of geographical locations, and using those words as repeating sets to re-render the original meaning. I have also reflected on lyrics as containing overused clichés, and looked at other clichéd and genred language.

ANNA McKERROW

LONDON, 2018

NÖTES ON THE PÖEMS

GIRLS, GIRLS, GIRLS

For this piece I cut up the lyrics to the title song of the album with a summary of Laura Mulvey's famous essay *Visual Pleasure and Narrative Cinema*. In the video for *Girls, Girls, Girls*, Mötley Crüe ride around LA on Harley Davidson motorbikes, catcalling and harassing women on the street before ending up in a strip bar where they watch the women dance and strip. The song details the various international strip clubs that the band has visited.

It seems entirely appropriate to deconstruct Crue's patriarchal looking-at-women by cutting their record of looking with Mulvey's critique of the male gaze.

FÖRWARD MY MAIL TÖ ME IN HELL

I'm afraid that I couldn't resist the line in the song 'Wild Side' which runs 'Forward My Mail to Me in Hell'. There is nothing in my piece that is ostensibly about female empowerment, but email scams such as the by now classic Nigerian bank transfer hoax text used for this poem (found on http://hoax-slayer.com/nigerian-scam-examples.html) represent hacking as a disruptive anti-capitalist practice and therefore a usefully disruptive discourse at the textual level.

Despite their 'bad boy' image and general revilement in the press at the height of their popularity, Mötley Crüe were living the capitalist dream of being paid extremely well for producing popular content within a patriarchal industry which reinforced traditional gender roles. They provided culture with a focus it could, at surface level, disapprove of, whilst remain happy that norms of sexual exploitation would remain normalised and, even, glamourised, in their million-selling albums, tours and videos.

Interestingly, mentions of the patriarchal Father as well as Mother Mary intersperse with Corporations in this piece, reflecting the power of institutions both religious and commercial present in both lyric and hoax text.

[ÄLL IN] THE NAME ÖF THE FATHER, BÖNËS, & ÄPPLE PIE TATTÖO

In my initial experiments with the song lyrics in *Girls, Girls, Girls* I took only the words present in the song and sought to rearrange them into pieces reflecting empowerment for women rather than sexual objectification. However, I had only limited success with that approach. This piece managed to emerge from the song 'All In The Name Of' which begins with the line 'She's only fifteen: she's the reason that I can't sleep'. However, it's not an empowering piece by any stretch of the imagination: more of a reflection of a teen girl's struggle in a world obsessed with controlling her and her fragile sexuality. In a similar way, I managed to make a poem about puppetry with 'Bones', but it may not be terribly effective. 'Apple Pie Tattoo' is another attempt at remaking a poem from the source text alone.

SHE PLAYS THE RÖLE OF A RÖVING MATRIARCH

For this series of poems I took the lyrics of 'Sumthin' for Nuthin' from the *Girls, Girls, Girls* album and used the Language is a Virus 'Mix Me With' online cutup generator to merge the lyrics with five different genre-based language samples. Each genre language word list contains a variety of what we might consider the most overused, clichéd and trite adverbs, adjectives and nouns in their specific lexicon, which seemed appropriate source material to use alongside lyrics that can fairly be judged as less than innovative or thoughtful.

As ever, by using the cutup process, I sought to re-juxtapose language from different sources to create moments of clarity, expose fresh meaning in the old meat and examine what happens when one set of clichés meets another.

The cutup generator can be found here: www.languageisavirus.com/mix-me-with/index.php#.Wu4ZnUxFzlU

FIVË YEARS UPTÖWN

The *Girls, Girls, Girls* album has a fascinating preponderance of place names in it, and repetition of various typical city zones such as Uptown, Downtown, Chinatown etc. I wanted to pattern a piece with a repeating pattern of locations and also a set of chosen, unoriginal and virtually meaningless adjectives used in the song such as 'sexy', 'wrong' and 'right' with the slightly more interesting 'punk', 'paper' and 'dead', which create a mood of street trash, decay and threat. The repeated locations typify, perhaps, the sameyness of cities when you're on tour, but also the repetitions symbolise the unoriginality of the way places are described; again, the limited text with a paucity of verve.

The obsession with locations reminded me of a terrible novella my uncle once wrote in which he noted the death of his female protagonist with a throwaway scene (and then had his male main character hit on her daughter at the graveside), but devoted two pages to a conversation with a cabbie in which the best route from London to Brighton, using only A roads, was debated. There is something so pathetically mundane in this kind of predilection for mapping lives to and from a place, while at the same time, not fully appreciating the real humans that populate those places and our lives. In the *Girls, Girls, Girls* album there is mention of a number of strip clubs in various cities the band has frequented, but no record of the women they found there, apart from that they were there, and they were sexually desirable. The women were not people: they were commodities.

We must think how especially galling it is to be successfully objectified with such poor vocabulary.

The last section of this poem combines and recombines the text of the song into a number of linked statements, trying to storify the language in some way. All we get is a kind of noir-esque place where Sue, a professional woman, is unable to leave behind her 'Sexy Sue' identity.

YOU'RE ALL I(NCEL) NEED

To reach this poem I cut up the following article about the Incel community from Psychology Today https://www.psychologytoday.com/us/blog/minority-report/201804/the-incel-movement with the lyrics of 'You're All I Need', a song about a man who kills a woman he is obsessed with. Lines such as the following are self-explanatory: 'You're all I need, make you only mine/ I loved you so I set you free / I had to take your life/ You're all I need, you're all I need/ You're all I need, And I loved you so/ But you didn't love me'.

While I don't think the band necessarily identified with this point of view, they chose to write a fairly sympathetic ballad from the point of view of a murderer, silencing and to some degree shaming the female victim. Musically, it's an affecting song which intends to invoke sympathy for the man with its sad chorus. Clearly, rejection is worse than death.

Girls, Girls, Girls

A reconstructive surgery for misogyny in 8 songs

BÖNËS

My downtown, downtown, down in the town, in London
Or Persia; my dreams come through a puppet.

my spoon dreams come through a puppet.
my glass dreams come through a puppet.
my silver dreams come through a puppet.
my London dreams come through a puppet.
my Persia dreams come through a puppet.

I pay for puppets to line dance fast
ya, ya, ya, ya! Trash style.

My spoon bones burn downtown.
My glass bones burn downtown.
My silver bones burn downtown.
My London bones burn downtown.
My Persia bones burn downtown.

The seams! The style! In my dreams,
In my dreams your spoon finds my bones.

In my dreams your extra bones find my child.
I'm silver, I'm a silver Jesus, Doctor

In my dreams your spoon finds my bones.
In my dreams your glass finds my bones.
In my dreams your silver finds my bones.
In my dreams your London finds my bones.
In my dreams your Persia finds my bones.

I'm never going back to dancing
I'm dancing in my dreams.

In my dreams your spoon bones find my child.
In my dreams your glass bones find my child.
In my dreams your silver bones find my child.
In my dreams your London bones find my child.
In my dreams your Persia bones find my child.

APPLË PIE TATTÖO

I tattooed her.
Just a few words and her story was
told; pride, a kiss, a town
a road. A bad boy.

(The glass!
The Chevrolet! The lock up!
I make the alibis. A .38 hit the glove.
I got my finger hit.
We never tell.)

Her hand found mine.

Tell us, tell us, round and round.
There's a method to a tattoo.
I'll make toast; we'll make toast shapes,
Labour and promise words, drink,
Make apple pie.

I tattooed her daughter.
Entertain us, raise the glass.
The world is love! I'll make the toast.

Better a girl with pride and promise.

Mama found a few words.

But the girl is badass madness!

I fit the apple pie and Chevrolet with

different shapes. A cookie jar tattoo.

An apple pie tattoo.

We have a drink in the love seat.

There's a method to my labour; love and promise.

Make apple pie, make cookies.

Tell us, tell us, round and round.

Make apple pie, make cookies.

Tattoo round and round.

There's a method to a tattoo.

There's a method to my labour.

FIVE YEARS ÜPTÖWN

CHÄPTER ÖNE

Downtown Hong Kong is the paper neighbourhood

Uptown Hong Kong is the sexy neighbourhood

Sexy Hong Kong is the wrong neighbourhood

Punk Hong Kong is the right neighbourhood

Dead Hong Kong is the punk neighbourhood

Happy Hong Kong is the dead neighbourhood

Downtown China Town is the paper neighbourhood

Uptown China Town is the sexy neighbourhood

Sexy China Town is the wrong neighbourhood

Punk China Town is the right neighbourhood

Dead China Town is the punk neighbourhood

Happy China Town is the dead neighbourhood

CHAPTER TWO

Downtown Hong Kong is the paper neighbourhood

Downtown Hong Kong is the sexy neighbourhood

Downtown Hong Kong is the wrong neighbourhood

Downtown Hong Kong is the right neighbourhood

Downtown Hong Kong is the punk neighbourhood

Downtown Hong Kong is the dead neighbourhood

Downtown China Town is the paper neighbourhood

Downtown China Town is the sexy neighbourhood

Downtown China Town is the wrong neighbourhood

Downtown China Town is the right neighbourhood

Downtown China Town is the punk neighbourhood

Downtown China Town is the dead neighbourhood

Uptown Hong Kong is the sexy neighbourhood

Uptown Hong Kong is the wrong neighbourhood

Uptown Hong Kong is the right neighbourhood

Uptown Hong Kong is the punk neighbourhood

Uptown Hong Kong is the dead neighbourhood

Uptown Hong Kong is the happy neighbourhood

Uptown China Town is the paper neighbourhood

Uptown China Town is the sexy neighbourhood

Uptown China Town is the wrong neighbourhood

Uptown China Town is the right neighbourhood

Uptown China Town is the punk neighbourhood

Uptown China Town is the dead neighbourhood

Sexy Hong Kong is the sexy neighbourhood

Sexy Hong Kong is the wrong neighbourhood

Sexy Hong Kong is the right neighbourhood

Sexy Hong Kong is the punk neighbourhood

Sexy Hong Kong is the dead neighbourhood

Sexy Hong Kong is the happy neighbourhood

Sexy China Town is the paper neighbourhood
Sexy China Town is the sexy neighbourhood
Sexy China Town is the wrong neighbourhood
Sexy China Town is the right neighbourhood
Sexy China Town is the punk neighbourhood
Sexy China Town is the dead neighbourhood

Punk Hong Kong is the paper neighbourhood
Punk Hong Kong is the sexy neighbourhood
Punk Hong Kong is the wrong neighbourhood
Punk Hong Kong is the right neighbourhood
Punk Hong Kong is the punk neighbourhood
Punk Hong Kong is the dead neighbourhood

Punk China Town is the paper neighbourhood
Punk China Town is the sexy neighbourhood
Punk China Town is the wrong neighbourhood
Punk China Town is the right neighbourhood
Punk China Town is the punk neighbourhood
Punk China Town is the dead neighbourhood

Dead Hong Kong is the paper neighbourhood
Dead Hong Kong is the sexy neighbourhood
Dead Hong Kong is the wrong neighbourhood
Dead Hong Kong is the right neighbourhood
Dead Hong Kong is the punk neighbourhood
Dead Hong Kong is the dead neighbourhood

Dead China Town is the paper neighbourhood

Dead China Town is the sexy neighbourhood

Dead China Town is the wrong neighbourhood

Dead China Town is the right neighbourhood

Dead China Town is the punk neighbourhood

Dead China Town is the dead neighbourhood

Happy Hong Kong is the paper neighbourhood

Happy Hong Kong is the sexy neighbourhood

Happy Hong Kong is the wrong neighbourhood

Happy Hong Kong is the right neighbourhood

Happy Hong Kong is the punk neighbourhood

Happy Hong Kong is the dead neighbourhood

Happy China Town is the paper neighbourhood

Happy China Town is the sexy neighbourhood

Happy China Town is the wrong neighbourhood

Happy China Town is the right neighbourhood

Happy China Town is the punk neighbourhood

Happy China Town is the dead neighbourhood

CHÄPTER TWÖ

Downtown Hong Kong is the paper neighbourhood

Uptown Hong Kong is the paper neighbourhood

Sexy Hong Kong is the paper neighbourhood

Punk Hong Kong is the paper neighbourhood

Dead Hong Kong is the paper neighbourhood

Happy Hong Kong is the paper neighbourhood

Downtown China Town is the paper neighbourhood

Uptown China Town is the paper neighbourhood

Sexy China Town is the paper neighbourhood

Punk China Town is the paper neighbourhood

Dead China Town is the paper neighbourhood

Happy China Town is the paper neighbourhood

Downtown Hong Kong is the sexy neighbourhood

Uptown Hong Kong is the sexy neighbourhood

Sexy Hong Kong is the sexy neighbourhood

Punk Hong Kong is the sexy neighbourhood

Dead Hong Kong is the sexy neighbourhood

Happy Hong Kong is the sexy neighbourhood

Downtown China Town is the sexy neighbourhood

Uptown China Town is the sexy neighbourhood

Sexy China Town is the sexy neighbourhood

Punk China Town is the sexy neighbourhood

Dead China Town is the sexy neighbourhood

Happy China Town is the sexy neighbourhood

Downtown Hong Kong is the wrong neighbourhood

Uptown Hong Kong is the wrong neighbourhood

Sexy Hong Kong is the wrong neighbourhood

Punk Hong Kong is the wrong neighbourhood

Dead Hong Kong is the wrong neighbourhood

Happy Hong Kong is the wrong neighbourhood

Downtown China Town is the wrong neighbourhood

Uptown China Town is the wrong neighbourhood

Sexy China Town is the wrong neighbourhood

Punk China Town is the wrong neighbourhood

Dead China Town is the wrong neighbourhood

Happy China Town is the wrong neighbourhood

Downtown Hong Kong is the right neighbourhood

Uptown Hong Kong is the right neighbourhood

Sexy Hong Kong is the right neighbourhood

Punk Hong Kong is the right neighbourhood

Dead Hong Kong is the right neighbourhood

Happy Hong Kong is the right neighbourhood

Downtown China Town is the right neighbourhood

Uptown China Town is the right neighbourhood

Sexy China Town is the right neighbourhood

Punk China Town is the right neighbourhood

Dead China Town is the right neighbourhood

Happy China Town is the right neighbourhood

Downtown Hong Kong is the punk neighbourhood

Uptown Hong Kong is the punk neighbourhood

Sexy Hong Kong is the punk neighbourhood

Punk Hong Kong is the punk neighbourhood

Dead Hong Kong is the punk neighbourhood

Happy Hong Kong is the punk neighbourhood

Downtown China Town is the punk neighbourhood

Uptown China Town is the punk neighbourhood

Sexy China Town is the punk neighbourhood

Punk China Town is the punk neighbourhood

Dead China Town is the punk neighbourhood

Happy China Town is the punk neighbourhood

Downtown Hong Kong is the dead neighbourhood

Uptown Hong Kong is the dead neighbourhood

Sexy Hong Kong is the dead neighbourhood

Punk Hong Kong is the dead neighbourhood

Dead Hong Kong is the dead neighbourhood

Happy Hong Kong is the dead neighbourhood

Downtown China Town is the dead neighbourhood

Uptown China Town is the dead neighbourhood

Sexy China Town is the dead neighbourhood

Punk China Town is the dead neighbourhood

Dead China Town is the dead neighbourhood

Happy China Town is the dead neighbourhood

CHAPTER THREE

Neighbourhood professional Sue shot a man.

Sexy Sue shot a man in Hong Kong.

Neighbourhood professional Sexy Sue never mattered to you.

Happy Sue was professional from the start.

Sexy Neighbourhood professional Sue shot a man in China Town.

Uptown Hong Kong is the punk neighbourhood.

Downtown China Town is the dead neighbourhood.

Neighbourhood professional Sue took the mark.

Sexy Sue missed the dead.

The neighbourhood never mattered to you.

Sexy Sue, Neighbourhood professional, missed the mark.

Neighbourhood professional Sue was bad from the start.

Sexy Hong Kong is the right neighbourhood.

Downtown China Town is the wrong neighbourhood.

Sexy Sue is a punk.

Uptown Hong Kong never mattered to you.

Uptown Hong Kong was bad from the start.

Neighbourhood professional Sue shot a neighbourhood.

Sexy neighbourhood professional Sue never mattered to punk.

Sexy Sue is dead.

Sue was bad from the start.

Professional Sue hit the mark from the start.

Happy Hong Kong Sue missed the neighbourhood.

Downtown Hong Kong never mattered to you.

Downtown Hong Kong was bad from the start.

The neighbourhood was bad from the start.

The neighbourhood was uptown.

Sexy Sue shot a neighbourhood in China Town.

Neighbourhood professional Sue was not a punk.

China Town was dead from the start.

China Town was punk from the start.

China Town was happy dead.

Uptown Hong Kong shot a man.

Uptown Hong Kong was professional.

Happy neighbourhood professional Sue never mattered to punk.

Happy neighbourhood professional Sue never mattered.

Neighbourhood professional Sue never mattered.

Sexy Sue was dead, downtown.

GIRLS, GIRLS, GIRLS

1.

part of wills beautiful

but and mockingly and of

cinema builds

those in

cinema,

they're the

patriarchal unconscreen.

Further asks that since

desires of Scarlett must bearer of cinema,

Rhett

hides between   Mulvey argues

that maker of grease

in

Ft. Laura Mulvey's

asks threat by

head stands in cinema, Rhett is

whole with a story

You

know she ideas objects, I wonder if

her

place as

she image when has

    behind

      of

      cinema builds

      Rhett

    must be

    very

integrated.

Tattle of woman   stately the approach

    at the objects and asks they're male-protagonist

      the best

    with

a

window.

    This

phanta

at by menage

the objects

a definite battle of desires on screen. Furtherefore

did me

    prevailinguistic

styles

    are theoristic common

    with the objects, I kept returning   an as well as that

    I

      need e news

In the

news

In the photos, and,

    second, secretly paradox"

    This a decidedly women paradox"

       can

    between this phanta

at Tattle of   cinema,

Rhett, and, secretly patriarchy which is

to make me

tight and Rhett

 his

    structure of those Frenchies laws

     with the

audiences see in

mains female presentation

     in theoristic styles on

screen. Further,

bound by remember

the protagonist Lauderdale

Girls, Girls,

    Girls, Girls, Girls, Girls, Girls, Girls, Girls, Girls,

    Girls, Girls, Girls,

Girls,

     Girls, Girls, Girls, Girls,

    Girls,

    Dancin' down to

Mulvey's and

active

which mainstreated interested

in the

approach

between screen.

     Mulvey

fingers in mainstream

film

  takingly

   and narration

of desire of media generative/male

    presentify,

     woman's that

      must between the

example)

woman stars, the patriarchal unconscreen.

Gone attempts the

     objects, I kept returning

   has beautiful

Mulvey begins female protagonist with a good good with a

  good with whole

on

   Sunset Strip

Girls, Girls, Girls,

Girls,

Girls, Girls,

  Girls,

Girls, Girls,

   Girls, Girls, Girls, Girls, Girls,

Girls, Girls, Girls, Girls,

2.

   Friday night

of, because

      what

      is to be

  worldly, and source of insipid decency.

   Yet respect

world I needed by the photos, a

  men's

    education for womance for me, I'll keep you

   read the

    one I mean

     Crazy Horse, Paris,

  France

On Halloween and outward observances,

because in

this

   to be really is.

  So they

reputation,

I'll keep you overemonies,
    and they're
    those

    Girls, Girls, Girls,
  Girls,
Girls,
Girls, Girls,
    Girls, Girls, Girls, Girls, Girls, Girls
  Long the behaviour must on
  his class of greason
    his own
world really is.
  So the
    system
      of mind;
      for me, I'll keep
you really is. So they reputation of any kind
        is to be read
that where I mean

      Crazy Horse, Paris, Frances, because that I have best when
    the whole
  behaviour and
can brave
behaviour and source one off the

best
   when
lost
  can brave
among
legs
   and outward
observance one I
    mean

    Crazy Horse, Paris, France one I mean

Crazy Horse, Paris, France one the virtue depending
  well produce of its
throne among legs
and outward for
it
 natural
rewards
only a kind
is virtue, arose
from a cause indispensable as indispensable Arch
   Girls, Girls, Girls, Girls, Girls, Girls,
    Girls, Girls,
 Dancin' down on
know she did me

Well proper

when

lost can brave behaviour and outward

observance

one

the one among

womance

Forget

to

be world I

am

conduct, depravity,

for

reputation she regard

observe they reputation

of mind;

for reputation of

any kind

is virtue

of

grease

in the

opinion of

mind; for unless about beat

On Halloween better — are mistaken. This

own on

of mind; for

reputation, indispensable as indispensable Arch

Girls ya just needed by

a

kind is been

denied. But when she really is. So

    the

    system

    of

      female depends only

a kind is built on

    know she read they reputation for reputation, indulgence one among legs

and the one though men's principal duty, for me, I'll

    keep you overemonies, became

      of her contrary

    to eat

On

    Hallowed

      up

ever

    be

really

is. So the

    grave you really is.

So

they reputation of her convinced to virtue off the underlying

    on

know the one among

    legs and

   can never be

really is. So they

  reputation of men better —are mistaken. It

is pure. Friday night

    My motive

is

built

  on Sunset Strip

 Girls, Girls,

Girls, Girls,

    Girls, Girls, Girls, Girls,

     Girls, Girls, Girls, Girls,

    Girls, Girls, Girls, Girls, Girls, Girls,

FÖRWARD MY MAIL TO ME IN HËLL

        be
absolutely not in your Banks and fine-tuned into
        your yesterday's
        cash lodgements

I am proposings for now.

        You
have
        absolutely
    not
    and money
that the
        Wild
        side
    for
        the
    son on the
        contained in heaven
Plead
then hell

Kneel down

to gain.

I carry

   be a ride

  on the

modality.

 Puppets as

Bearer Bonds and fine-tuned to ass   on then, hell

Kneel down

to your

for us.

      60 % of this transfer of this money, which

is in anticipation was carried out

withdraw

all documents

  and

  onward my

mail to miss this project.

We not want to the

  Petroleum

Corp.,

to

    the Federal Government Parastatals, forwarded to

Mr.

    Patrice Miller,

Presidential that midnight

    Papa won't

be the nearest

you are

not easy to cover

invoiced to

a

foreign firm

    in this

    transaction,

as soon as

   possible funds

   transfer of this

money

would give us make formation of the whole

future.

    It

   might be home tonight

Papa won't be

incurred during time on

  the whole future.

International Petroleum Corporational   Petroleum Corporational Petroleum
Corporational expect you

10% of

the wild side

Wild

side

    Our father

 Long lost

in the wild side

Wild side

    Wild side

Wild side

    Wild

side

  Wild

  side

Wild

side   Holy Mary

   Mother or not want

   to the

   Federal Government Parastatals

$ 21.5Million,

we

   would be

  for

  us.

Your Full Name,

  Company's Name,

    Company's

  Name, Company's Name, Company's Name, Company's

    Name, Company's Name

– You must

    kill

Thy kingdom

come by.

    as possible funds transaction,

carry my

  crucifix

  Petroleum Corp., of

153

  East L.A.

    at midnight

 Papa won't be

the

nearest possible

funds

 to a

foreign firm in this

project.

We not international Petroleum Corporation

of the

wild

side

Wild side

Wild side

Wild

side

Wild

side

Wild

side

Wild

side

Wild side

Wild side

Wild

side

Wild side

Wild

side Holy Mary

Mother

bank account Number-

881-631-410-574, specially

elected government Of Nigeria

and disappeared completely.

The

Father

Long lost in anti –

(ALL IN) THË NAME ÖF THE FATHER

In the name of control I dirty my soul
In the name of control I dirty my soul
In the name of control I dirty my soul

I try to sleep, daddy, but
I'm pretty all in;
I try like hell, but nothing.

Dirty name, candy name, pretty pretty
Dirty name, candy name, pretty pretty

You say I'm fifteen, I'm out of control.
I say the world's the reason, the world's hell,
But, you know, daddy says to me,

Hell's innocent. The world's innocent.

You know you can

Try.
Try.
Try.

Brings me magazines

Like they ain't the reason

Dirty name, candy name, pretty pretty

Dirty name, candy name, pretty pretty

But daddy is control

And the world is control

And nothing I say is legal.

I can't sleep; my soul is in hell.

My soul is innocent.

My name is pretty.

I am nothing.

I

Try.

Try.

Try.

I'd sell my soul for control.

SHE PLAYS THE RÖLE OF A RÖVING MATRIARCH

THEMED CÜTÜP 1 : FAIRY TALE

the ruby thorn day
        matriarch satisfaction
and an elfin guaranteed plays
I'm princesses, hobgoblins
        the guaranteed transforming satisfaction
practice in practice on the slipper

sumthin' enchantments slumber the nuthin'
good pixie easy nuthin' queens
banshees thorny orphans twinkling
money crossroads in nevermirror ogre towers

fauns rich to seconds shimmer
        Lorelei sounds free
needle for your unicorn, your orphan sprite
deed my satisfaction in twinkled fancy itch
twice love on and stitch

Nuthin' the transformations

faun's courtiers cauldron

a dormouse sees Gigolo visions

I'm rose crack out

enchantments aglitter love gingerbread

her roving where seconds break in practice

      matriarch door time

iridescently my fairy plays dormouse break

treat your courtiers the best overtime

free good shimmer   the easy needle transforms my 16 faun

never is ruby to nymph's goblet

to seelie slumber buried treasures slipped to twilight

and at old spring crossroads

changeling toadstool/toadstools potion out

      the nymph's matriarch

easy 16 centuries for queen's price cloaks

nuthin' cold

mirror subterranean crazy twinkle

THEMED CÜTUP 2: RÖMANCE

late fed   deep unrequited

the wraps forgiven loves

my rides shiver helm

Name your trail   the unlocked snuggle

strained aristocrats free the coiled double day priest

hungering rescuing I'm gorgeous working gazing stitch

and sounds alluring never rolling

exalted satisfaction hauls lady to the scandal clock

kilted heartbroken enchants scratch spark

impetuous stitch of mistress women

matriarch wish skill staring the trail

plump love plays sumthin' savouring –

strength strained ghost sumthin' –

exalts to watch a hungry sumthin' –

stir tragic horse held merciless tempts a responsive fall

practice stagger lovely whispering

rescued my watch a for swirling scratch

covered coaxed and overtime

Paris wrap comely weds

I'm inviting spring

overwhelms electrifies drinks wishes

ruin my plays holy matrimony crash

rush her rings trail   stretching the wedding bride

grazes revelries drown pinched rhapsody restrain

marquis in best fluttered grace to lifted satin

a moment rushing in   Dubonnet day

skin double toy

feral man swirled good smoky transporting sobs

broken coax is for free

love jolts 63   smells   tumbles

matriarch gave jewels

royal held well-mannered white dove so

pest together pay desired in staggers

exulted temptation target seduction braced

THEMED CÜTÜP 3: SCIENCE FICTIÖN

easy trade route   foolish nuthin' warp drives for galactic scale

toy   an old invader guaranteed

63 temporal anomaly rings invent plutonium sunspots

time-free sounds for cold radio waves to Deneb

leave in spring dropped days   rings trade

tesseract guaranteed   nuthin' overtime

spring vaporizes target brown dwarves to borgs paradox

never such proxima centauri rich happy money   laser blasters

I'm double sumthin'

good microsecond for break

crack call scratch telepathy

zap 63 pigfolk

captain heisenberg uncertainty principle

roving spring planet starbunny

dark matter spamdroids and betelgeuse

living ship teleports irregular galaxies to you   solar sails double

happy satisfaction clone

Dubonnet signals type 0 civilization

acidfruit fancy charged particles to her probes

you bring good   guaranteed

bring its dream recorder unlocked

leave the easy metamaterial

overtime androids delta 42   mark metamaterials

                              watch atmospheric pressure

                              scratch money crack flops

                              tesseract in the positronic network

Nuthin' telekinetic

shock itch jar   world ethane

slipped engine teacher's supercomputer

it's me rangers

diamond your saturn

THEMED CÜTUP 4: SPÖRTS

back the sumo

and winner me

disadvantage a locker room   dark manoeuvred Dubonnet   things cross

squash handball gully

furlong coffin corner rings

umpire roving yards stitch

guaranteed plays mulligan backlift for the battle

I'm your vuvuzela   hack slipped stick   shot it

foolish for kickoff

block rallies disadvantage

knock the pinch hitter on stealing   home triple play

     matriarch points deduction behind money

horseback 16 unlocked   bring karate shock spot

     break in play

I'll Target for outs

I'll batter never

good call   offensive canoe

manoeuvre   tee dive old manoeuvre s

gigolo shot breaks the circle

quiver visiting caddy clubhouse   seed

short stop jockey defensive wall

nuthin' pro easy for war chest

fancy trophy hole-in-one

the plan plays at overtime

skiing triumph a screwball appeal   goalie crack

maneuver   sounds late   see it's perfect

score curls to clock for crack   and it's stealing money

batter up   clock turns seconds   target   foolish backlift

seconds   Dubonnet

THEMED CÜTÜP 5: BACCHANALIA

on call shock entheogens

target her money crack   gingerbread was sweet time

entheogenic in ballgowns

entheogenic feast never danced in the consumed

scourge crack a vermilion price toy

the flute slipped color uninhibitedly to vermilion

sumthin' 16 see liberation seconds

best watch teachers the chant rocks

the easy roving mushroom

indulging madness in drumming uninhibited   a double nuthin' call

rich sounds for sweet days scourge

good sweet guaranteed revelry deed

itch the orgy   Dubonnet seduction

leave free carnivalesque orgy masks

cinnamon guaranteed chanted day possession

I'm for fragrant consuming   dancing drum dance

sumthin' hobgoblin sumthin' seduction uninhibited dancing drumming for

possession

revelries guaranteed pagan drums

nuthin' torches feasts   overtime stitch

watch scourges taboos   nuthin' indulges good my rituals

late on bacchanalia drumming

drugs   chants   cold azure dances bacchanalia crack

diamond for things hallucinations the needle

mystical needle got sumthin' of the teacher's

dionysian slipped cold faun

mushrooms trances myrrh taboos

azure satyrs practice consuming and

rituals bride festivities

free trance the fauns' silk needle

crack such merrymaking   orphan the deed torment

pay money   indulge stitch orgies overtime

invoke intoxicate happy

invoke cardamom

YÖU'RE ALL I(NCEL) NËED

short your comic

forums knife isolation

Pokemon Year 40 profile

oftentimes endure you

only we only

        and many you 30

        hobbies of a guess

        pressure not height

shaming out online demographic sexually in acne

and you you you're on friends video name

physical due a tears

     his societal sense like made by created

But acceptance   on my cold to you

And love's all lips   only we only

But need   you're 40

Incel

          I reflect

this inept Warcraft love

happy love start for breath marriage

popular situations character sex new character

Combine profile Faced changed

need feels   eyes social

    away all mine world and Virgin objective

be better

blood make self own

condemnation inadequate defective share shift

retitle social to home   only we only

www.ingramcontent.com/pod-product-compliance
Lightning Source LLC
LaVergne TN
LVHW061258060426
835508LV00015B/1415